NEUROSIS
A SMALL BIG BOOK

RAJ DOCTOR

Raj Doctor is a trained
Architect, town-planner and management expert.
He is an international not-for-profit organization expert
Currently he lives in Jaipur. INDIA.

Also by
Raj Doctor

Melancholy of Innocence, Romantic Novel
Ashtavakra – Dialogues with King Janak
Potpourri of AMOUR – Melange (A-Z Series)
Smorgasbord of Eros
Panoply of Ode
What is Human Rights?
NEUROSIS – A small BIG book

ISBN-13: 978-1546829294
ISBN-10: 1546829296
This book has been assigned a CreateSpace ISBN

Printed and bound at CreateSpace

Authored and Edited by: Raj Doctor

Font Calibri (Body) 8, 11, 16, 22

Dedicated to

To those who think
People suffering from NEUROSIS
Need treatment
And they forget that
They are the ones
Who are neurotic
And require treatment...

Contents

Preface

The thought of writing this small BIG book came when I realized the effects of subject to the word "neurosis" and what it means.

It led me to introspect a lot and find the state at which a person is in compared to the world that calls someone neurotic.

I did not want to write something technical and sort of a research paper, I wanted to keep it simple, yet communicate what I felt about the word "neurosis"

So here is my brief *"A small BIG book on NEUROSIS."*

I hope the readers like it.

Raj Doctor
India 2017

Raj Doctor

WHO IS NEUROTIC?

Do you know who is neurotic?

Is it the one who believes in
TRUE PURE AGAPE LOVE?

Or

The one who doesn't LOVE?

DEFINTION

Neurosis is
Repression of LOVE
Its psychosexual development
Resulting in formation of behavior
Or symptoms as a result
Of feeling fear, anxiety, depression
Fleeing from people who LOVE them
Seeking security through others
Mainly family, friends and colleagues

THE KING AND QUEEN

A magician came to a medieval kingdom
And chanted a few mantras
Threw powder dust into the well and said
"Whoever drinks this water will go mad"

Now there were only two wells in the town
One inside the palace and the other in the town

Within two days - the whole town became mad
Except the king and queen who had that special well

By evening King and Queen got scared
Because they heard a rumor
That "King and Queen have become mad"

Actually, the whole town was mad except them
"What to do?" they discussed...

"To remain alive we have to drink the water from that well
Otherwise these mad people will kill us
Thinking we are mad"

So they went and secretly drank the well's water
And both the king and queen started dancing
While returning back to the palace...

The majority of populations of
The town celebrated with joy
They shouted slogans:

"Long live the king
Long live the queen
They have become sane again"

DON'T COMPLAINT

For those who cannot LOVE
Don't complain
They have to live with neurosis
There is no other way to live in this society
The whole populace is neurotic
Everyone creates LOVE on their own
In their own minds and thoughts
No one actually LOVES anyone
So same way - be neurotic and live...
Don't complain
Neurosis in today's world is essential
(Sarcasm)

THE NEW NORMAL

Today, the neurotic mind is considered normal
That far the humans have moved away from
Nature, normal and LOVE

Knowledge drives people neurotic
Half knowledge in ignorant mind
That just finds truth in everything
Becomes completely neurotic

LOVE is the only thing that relaxes such neurosis

Raj Doctor

ULTRA ACTIVE

Neurosis means mind is ultra active
It is working over time, there is no rest
There is no time for LOVE

There is no freedom, there is no liberty
There is nothing like soaring in the skies
Or wings in flight
Until the being is subjected by LOVE
The burden of neurosis ever increases

14

LEVELS OF NEUROSIS

The best example of
LEVELS of neurosis is

YOU feel one thing
You think another
You speak something
YOU write something else
YOU act totally different

OR - Are consistent in you
Across all the above five categories?

There are many combinations emerging out of
The above five categories
The more inconsistency you have
Across them
The more neurotic you are

LOVE flowing across
All of the above categories consistently is normal
That is No Neurosis

COMPLETE NEUROSIS

With complete neurosis
The natural being is gone
You become a false *'being'*
And you also become
Afraid even to think about
The natural being you were

Because

The moment you feel
Your innocence & LOVE again
The whole society, world
Will be against YOU
And you fear that
You think it is better to
Follow society than be
Your own true self and
Be called neurotic

REAL CAUSE

The real cause of neurosis is
Because of LOVE energy
The repression of LOVE causes neurosis
Are you the one who represses your LOVE or other's LOVE?
By the way...
The former is more neurotic than the latter

LEADS TO...

Neurosis leads a person to tell lies
Neurosis leads a person to psychosis
To split personalities
Neurosis leads a person to
Live one life within and another life outside
The person suffering neurosis is
The one who least knows about its neurosis
One needs to deeply accept LOVE
To solve the problem of neurosis

COUNSELLERS & PSYCHIATRIST

But if you are neurotic,
You are struggling to be YOU
That time, never go to counseling,
Never go to a psychiatrist
(They will work as enemies of humanity)

I will explain you why

They want to do things to put you right back
In this neurotic society
They are the silent agent of maintaining a neurotic society
They fit YOU into a value system,
Morals, integrity, virtues society
That is the only way neurosis can survive

ARROGANCE

Now the same 95% of the world
The majority who do not believe in LOVE
Who laugh at LOVE
Have the arrogance to cast
Everyone who believes in LOVE as "neurotic"

TODAY'S WORLD

99% of world falsely assumes that
They are mostly normal
And those who are neurotic
-    The Remaining 1% are LOVERS

Now with that awareness
Relook at the state of world is today
On the brink of extinction!

WORLD DIVIDED

The rift in the world
Is between those who LOVE
And those who don't LOVE
You introspect and know which
Side of divide you belong to?
I won't say who belongs where and
Who is neurotic?

STATE OF THE WORLD

That is the state of the world today
The whole world is neurotic to certain degrees
That is why they see a human believing in LOVE "INSANE"
Hence Jesus was crucified
Hence Mansoor was lynched
And hence we know
Majnun and Meera were stoned

VIOLENCE

If humans are kept away from LOVE
Humans will become negative,
Pessimistic, neurotic and angry
And the fall out of that would be
Violence of many sorts
That harms and hurts other
Living beings and creatures

See the state of planet earth today
You will know the cause of neurosis of humanity

MAJORITY

Majority of people are against LOVE
They are drunk with contaminated well of intelligence
(The King and Queen story)
Anyone who is not like them in the world
For them, anyone who does not think, speak, write like them
Is mad and neurotic and
They have to be punished, eliminated
Such are neurotic people

AWAKE OR ASLEEP

This world is full of neurotic people
If one person decides to wake up one's LOVE
You will be thought mad, mentally ill
So better you go back to sleep knowing
The level of your intellectual neurosis

Neurosis is the new truth of LIFE
(Sarcasm)

PERSONAS

Neurosis leads to a multiple personas disorder
The human with more personas,
Has MORE neurosis

The human with less personas,
Has LESS neurosis
The one with LESS neurosis
Are obviously LOVERS

MENTAL ILLNESS

The less said about
Mental illness the better
Just have a look around and
See the state where humans
Have obsessively brought
The world to the brink of extinction
Without knowing their own neurosis

These I am talking of 95% of
Human population who are those
Who strive to be intellectuals
To save the world in name of development
Now it is called "sustainable development"
(Sarcasm)

WELL OF LIFE

If you have drank from
The contaminated well called modern LIFE
You will suffer neurosis
Like the majority
And those who are not like the majority
Are labeled suffering from NEUROSIS

THOUGHTS

When there are fragments of thoughts
When mind over-works
Neurosis takes place

To rest that mind,
To rest neurosis
LOVE is a necessity

MIND

Neurosis is mind that affects the body

THINKING

Thinking is the basis of neurosis
That kills humanity and LOVE

CLARITY

When one cannot think clearly
When one cannot see clearly
When one feels confused
One keeps battling with oneself
One wants to be something, but one cannot be!
One wants LOVE, but one does not LOVE or get LOVE
One wants companionship, but one does not get it
One wants someone to understand, but one does not get one
Things are not clear in front of us
Such are the ways neurosis affects humans

MOTHER AND CHILD

A small child wanted to play with the sand on the beach
His mother said
"No! Don't play because
The sand is wet and you will spoil your clothes"
Then the small child wanted to go near the water.
His mother said
"No, absolutely not
It is slippery and you may fall there"
Then the child wanted to run and
Jump around and the mother said:
"No you may get lost in the crowd"
Then the child asked
For an ice cream because
The ice cream vendor was near
His mother said:
"No because that always creates
A problem with your throat
And it is bad for your health"
Then the child started playing with a girl
Making sand castles and Mother's said
"No, not at all,
Being with her is not good for you!"
And the child was upset and
Started rolling in mud, and crying

The mother turned to the person
Who was standing near by
"Have you seen such a neurotic child?
See how he suffers from neurosis?"

Lesson:
The child is not neurotic
The mother is neurotic

SEEDS OF NEUROSIS

When freedom is killed, neurosis is born
When someone is NOT allowed
To say "I LOVE YOU"
Neurosis is born on the one
Who is imposing those restrictions on LOVE

BIRTH

When a child is born
A child is a *'feeling being'*
S/he feels things...
When s/he starts behaving
To a particular society's ways
Neurosis steps in as
The mind steps in and
S/he loses the feeling part
The LOVE part disappears
Neurosis steps in

UNBRINGING

Humans are born for rearing
But wrong rearing causes neurosis

Human child is not allowed to be FREE
Child has to be conditioned, trained, and taught
That creates patterns of neurosis in every human
The society molds you
If you fit into the society mold
The neurotic society will not call you neurotic
If you do not fit into the society
The neurotic society will call you neurotic

Upbringing of a child
Brings up repression within the child
Don't do this, behave like this and behave like that
Those repressions are neurosis
The more you are exposed to those
The more neurotic you grow up to be

CHILDHOOD & YOUTH

Neurosis happens since childhood
But the conflict
The face of face battle with oneself
Is mostly faced during youth
It is the time when one wants LOVE, and
One is taught everything against LOVE
And youth becomes neurotic

GROWING UP

Growing up process makes everyone
Neurotic - obsessive about LIFE
Living, work, success, seeking meaning
Seeking answers, seeking identify
Seeking achievements,
Wealth, power, prestige, status
The list is endless...
They have forgotten their own LOVE within

Now who remembers LOVE?

Now just see the fun of the world
They who don't LOVE call others – Neurotic!
(Sarcasm)

CHAIN OF NEUROSIS

The chain of neurosis runs and amplifies
From one society to another
From one generation to another
LOVE is the only thing that
Cuts free the cycle of neurosis

CYCLE OF NEUROSIS

**Only the one who is sensitive
Thoughtful, caring, kind and LOVING
Is able to break free from the cycle of neurosis
LOVE is the first step out of neurosis**

FEAR

To look at neurosis is to look at the fear you are facing
To embrace the "something good"
That you fear
Heals neurosis

It's like someone loves you,
But you fear LOVE
Embrace the one who LOVES you
And neurosis disappears

AWARENESS

Just the awareness of knowing
What you dislike? What you fear?
Is the first step towards removing neurosis...

You need to cultivate that attention –
Energy to look at neurosis
And neurosis is gone

PERFECT

Everyone wants to be "perfect"
A slight tangent piece of paper on table is kept straight
Everyone is on the drive to be "perfect"

The respect one carries for others
For other individual – for each individual
And what respect they carry within
Is demolished by the vague idea of *perfection*
Everyone is trying to mold themselves to a standard
Standard of perfection
(Sarcasm)

QUEST FOR PERFECTION

In this quest for "perfection"
Humanity has destroyed the possibility of LOVE
Within individuals because they only see world
Within the chains they are tied to
The paths the herd is driven to
It is a factory supply line
And humans are raw materials
The final product is a standardized form
Be it type of education, type of look
The way we talk, the way we behave
Everything fits to some standard
(Sarcasm)

NATURE

"Denial of LOVE is crime against nature"
And
Nature will take its revenge its own way
The revenge results in world "neurosis"

FEAR OF LOVE

Neurosis creates fear of LOVE
But humans want to LOVE
So they try every way to dissipate their neurosis
By doing stupidest thing
Work, power, prestige, saving planet,
Human rights, feminism, equality, animal right
They try everything – except LOVE

Only LOVE gives you deep contentment
To cure human neurosis

BELIEF IN LOVE

Everyone who does not believe in LOVE
Everyone who practices LIFE without LOVE
Becomes neurotic to some extend

Now how to make them know without
Offending them, that
They are not practicing LOVE and
That is why they have neurosis
And they are neurotic

LOVE

Nobody teaches humans 'LOVE'
Humans are born natural
Real, normal beings with LOVE
LOVE inborn in their inner self

While growing humans learn
Varying degrees of neurosis
When they move away from inner LOVE
That is the way world kills LOVE sooner/ later

RULES

LOVE is not for someone
Who follows rules

The rules are created and imposed in
Neurotic societies

REAL NATURE

LOVE is your basic nature

When neurosis steps in
You start forgetting
Your real nature

The more you move farther away from LOVE
The more you are subjected to neurosis

REAL SELF AND REALITY

When your natural being is suppressed
The unnatural and unreal is imposed
This grows *"unreality"* is your mind

The wider this split between
Your real self and the reality
You are living in
Defines
The suffering of neurosis

INNER LOVE

The humans who completely forget
The importance of the inner LOVE
Has achieved complete neurosis

KABIR

Kabir says:
"I will tell you the truth"

I will tell you the truth

The less LOVE - means more mad
The more LOVE - means less mad

But the real world will call you

The less LOVE – means normal
The more LOVE – means mad

(Kabir uses the word **mad** in place of neurosis)

TRUTH OF NEUROSIS

If you understand the truth of Neurosis
And its association with LOVE,
One thing is certain
You will be considered mad

Once you listen to LOVE, you are at risk
You will understand the truth of life

If you fear LOVE, you will go back to sleep
The sleep of living dead
Like most of the society individuals

If you become aware and wake up
From LIFE to LOVE
You will be at risk from the society
Please do not blame LOVE
LOVE's duty was to tell you the truth
A LOVER will tell you the truth
I told you the truth of LOVE

WHAT IS NOT NEUROSIS

To fall in LOVE is not neurosis
To LOVE someone passionately, deeply
Is not neurosis

FREEDOM

A neurotic mind cannot say "YES"
To many things because
A neurotic mind cannot allow
Freedom to one's own self
How will it allow freedom to anyone?
How it will allow freedom to LOVE?

EGO

What LOVE does?
Fights with neurosis
EGO is the source of all neurosis
When in true LOVE,
EGO disappears
A human in LOVE is stable
A state very near to NO-neurosis

IGNORANCE

Neurosis is a perversion of EGO
Caused by ignorance
Gathering useless information

EGO says –
I am the center of universe
I am something,
Neurosis is born

LOVE kills that neurosis

"I"

The very assertion of "I" is neurosis
And LOVE is the only weapon against neurosis

LOVE truly deeply passionate
And LOVE will drop your "I"
LOVE will kill the "I"
And neurosis will disappear

Only when the neurosis goes
The "I" disappears and LOVE blooms

EPIDEMIC

With world moving away from LOVE
Neurosis has become an epidemic of
Vast proportions

With LOVE,
Accepting to being LOVED
And LOVING
You become natural again
You become innocent, pure
Like a river flowing into the ocean
Or the clouds floating in the sky
Or the winds passing the forest

THE MOUSE

Neurosis is the mouse

This mouse is the mind
Endlessly trying the dead end
Without learning that LOVE is the opening
LOVE is the cure

For Neurotic mind in neurosis
It is difficult to understand this very fact

Non-learning creates neurosis
Un-learning creates non-neurosis

**That is why LOVE is needed today
More than ever before**

MEDITATION

LOVE is the only meditation
Of the BELOVED
To moves away from neurosis

INNOCENCE

In LOVE, the being becomes innocent
The mind un-clutters, unlearns,
Experiences are digested into the being
The over load of thoughts disappear

INFORMATION

The mind is not able to digest the
Over-load of information in the Information Technology age
Information collected from everywhere - *social media*

LOVE means - there is no time to
Assimilate and digest useless information
You are not in the race,
You are not part of the herd
You are less neurotic

THE NEW NORMAL

It is not that a few humans are neurotic
The whole of humanity is neurotic
In the modern world
Neurosis is a new NORMAL

OBEDIENCE

When major part of beings are in bondage of obedience
Everyone cultivates a neurotic mind
Disobedience of any type is neurotic
For this neurotic group

DEATH OF NEUROSIS

A neurotic mind will never die,
It will grow more neurotic
No technique, no religion,
No spirituality, no meditation
Will cure your neurosis

BORN OUT OF LOVE

Because every human being is born out of LOVE
How much ever they try
Humans cannot fight LOVE
But when humans are told not to LOVE
LOVE is bad,
Humans become neurotic
They start fighting with themselves
They start fighting with the world

REPRESSION OF LOVE

Because of this repression of LOVE
Humans live in guilt
That guilt causes neurosis
The more humans stay away from LOVE
The more neurotic humans will become

POSSESSED

Modern human is possessed due to this neurosis
They are possessed to
Succeed, to earn money
To work, to save humanity –
All these are different forms of neurosis
But they do not know, they do not realize
That real possession to LOVE is eluded

If you are possessed to LOVE
Neurosis disappears

POWER GAME

There is a power struggle
By those who want humanity to dissipate
Their energies of LOVE to something else..

How can that happen?
When a person with an authority declines you
They do not allow you to do certain things
And one of that thing
– the most important thing
They do not allow you is

"LOVE"

CURE

Neurosis can be cured only
When you are one with yourself
You may ask
"How can one be ONE with oneself?"
LOVE is the only path
To achieve that

But you need not take that path deliberately
Then you will not find LOVE
Nor you will cure your neurosis

Just try to unlearn everything, and
Remove all your beliefs
The doors and windows and
Paths may open up to LOVE
Just wait for LOVE to come and happen
When it happens,
The cure of neurosis takes place

SOLUTION

So YOU are right
LOVE is the root problem

Give freedom to LOVE

No one will be neurotic in this world

HEALING

NEUROSIS IS HEALED

Once a human is in deep LOVE

That is the very life of human

Neurosis is healed